Donated by
Editorial Directions
in honor of
The Koutris Family
to the
Olive-Mary Stitt LMC
2003-2004

*"One must never, in one's own life, accept . . .
injustices as commonplace but must fight them
with all one's strength. This fight begins, however,
in the heart. . . ."*

—JAMES BALDWIN

JAMES BALDWIN: AFRICAN-AMERICAN WRITER AND ACTIVIST

BY DEBORAH CANNARELLA

Content Reviewer: Dr. David Leeming, Professor Emeritus,
University of Connecticut

The Child's World

Published in the United States of America by The Child's World®
PO Box 326
Chanhassen, MN 55317-0326
800-599-READ
www.childsworld.com

The Child's World®: Mary Berendes, Publishing Director
Editorial Directions, Inc.: E. Russell Primm and Emily Dolbear, Editors; Katie Marsico and
Elizabeth K. Martin, Editorial Assistants; Dawn Friedman, Photo Researcher; Linda S. Koutris,
Photo Selector; Kerry Reid, Fact Researcher; Susan Hindman, Copy Editor; Halley Gatenby,
Proofreader; Tim Griffin/IndexServ, Indexer; Vicki Fischman, Page Production

Cover photograph: James Baldwin in Paris in 1986 / © Peter Turnley/Corbis

Interior photographs ©: Nancy Kaye/AP/Wide World Photos: 6; AP/Wide World Photos: 29, 33, 34, 36; Yale
Collection of American Literature, Beinecke Rare Book & Manuscript Library: 10, 24, 27; Peter
Turnley/Corbis: 2; Corbis: 7, 11; Bettmann/Corbis: 8, 9, 12, 16–17, 18, 19, 20, 25, 28, 31 left, 32; Allen
Ginsberg/Corbis: 13; Joseph Schwartz Collection/Corbis: 15; Hulton Archive/Getty Images: 23, 31 right.

Library of Congress Cataloging-in-Publication Data
Cannarella, Deborah.
James Baldwin : African-American writer and activist / by Deborah Cannarella.
p. cm. — (Journey to freedom)
"An editorial directions book"—T.p. verso.
Includes index.
Contents: Native Son—Greenwich Village—An American in Paris—"Witness to the Truth"— Timeline.
ISBN 1-56766-531-4 (Library Bound : alk. paper)
1. Baldwin, James, 1924– —Juvenile literature. 2. Authors, American—20th century—Biography—Juvenile
literature. 3. Civil rights workers—United States—Biography—Juvenile literature. 4. African American
authors—Biography—Juvenile literature. [1. Baldwin, James, 1924– 2. Authors, American. 3. Civil rights
workers. 4. African Americans—Biography.] I. Title. II. Series.
PS3552.A45Z633 2003
818'.5409—dc21
2003004294

Contents

JAMES BALDWIN, SHOWN HERE IN 1982, WAS AN IMPORTANT AFRICAN-AMERICAN WRITER AND ACTIVIST. HE WAS STRONGLY COMMITTED TO THE CIVIL RIGHTS MOVEMENT.

Native Son

"I want to be an honest man," James Baldwin said, "And I want to be a good writer." He met both of these goals. By always telling the truth about himself—and the world around him—he became one of the most important writers of his time.

James Arthur Jones was born on August 2, 1924, in Harlem, an **African-American** neighborhood in New York City. His mother was Emma Berdis Jones. He never knew his real father. When James was three years old, his mother married David Baldwin, a factory worker from Louisiana. David was also a **preacher.** David and Emma had eight children. The youngest was born the day that David died.

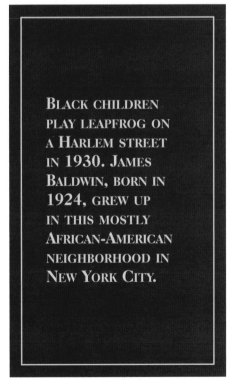

BLACK CHILDREN PLAY LEAPFROG ON A HARLEM STREET IN 1930. JAMES BALDWIN, BORN IN 1924, GREW UP IN THIS MOSTLY AFRICAN-AMERICAN NEIGHBORHOOD IN NEW YORK CITY.

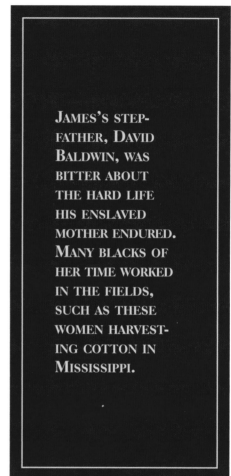

David Baldwin's mother had been a slave. He was born a "free man." But David was angry at the cruel way that white people still treated African-Americans. His hard life made him bitter. He did not want his children to play games or listen to music. He told James that he was the ugliest child he had ever seen. James often cried himself to sleep. He grew up believing that David Baldwin was his real father. He did not learn the truth until he was a teenager.

James later understood and forgave his stepfather. But he grew up afraid of him, and he hid in his books. He read books "like they were some sort of weird food," he later said. One of his favorites was a book about **slavery** in the South called *Uncle Tom's Cabin*, by Harriet Beecher Stowe.

James also loved to write. He wrote stories and poems on grocery bags when his family could not afford to buy paper. By age nine, he wrote a short play. His teacher, Orilla Miller, took him to see a play in a theater for the first time—even though his stepfather didn't approve.

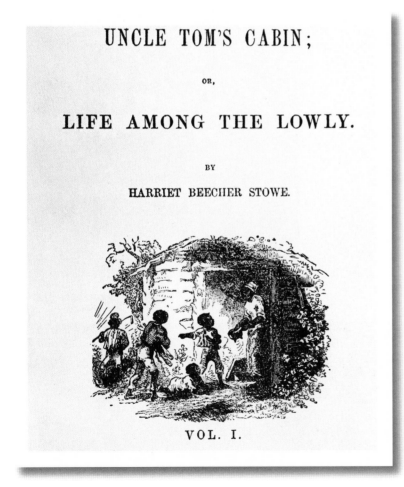

UNCLE TOM'S CABIN;

OR,

LIFE AMONG THE LOWLY.

BY

HARRIET BEECHER STOWE.

VOL. I.

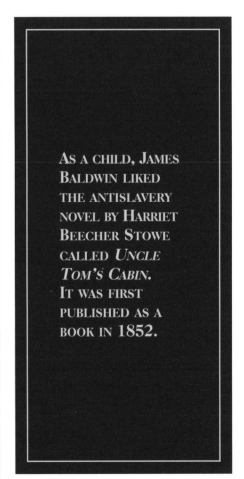

AS A CHILD, JAMES BALDWIN LIKED THE ANTISLAVERY NOVEL BY HARRIET BEECHER STOWE CALLED *UNCLE TOM'S CABIN*. IT WAS FIRST PUBLISHED AS A BOOK IN 1852.

James was shy and small in size. The other kids made fun of him and called him Popeyes. But his teachers knew he had a talent for writing. Countee Cullen, a well-known African-American poet, was one of his teachers at Frederick Douglass Junior High School. He taught James about Langston Hughes, Arna Bontemps, and other black writers of the time.

A teacher named Herman Porter asked James to join the school newspaper, the *Douglass Pilot.* James wrote **essays** about the history and the people of Harlem. Porter also took James downtown on the bus to visit the New York Public Library. James had never seen so many books! After that, James often went there alone—even though he did not always feel welcome in this mostly white section of the city.

POET AND NOVELIST COUNTEE CULLEN, SHOWN HERE IN A PORTRAIT FROM 1925, TAUGHT JAMES BALDWIN AT FREDERICK DOUGLASS JUNIOR HIGH SCHOOL IN NEW YORK CITY.

AS A STUDENT, JAMES BALDWIN OFTEN TRAVELED FROM HIS HOME IN HARLEM TO
MIDTOWN MANHATTAN'S NEW YORK PUBLIC LIBRARY, SHOWN HERE IN THE 1920S.

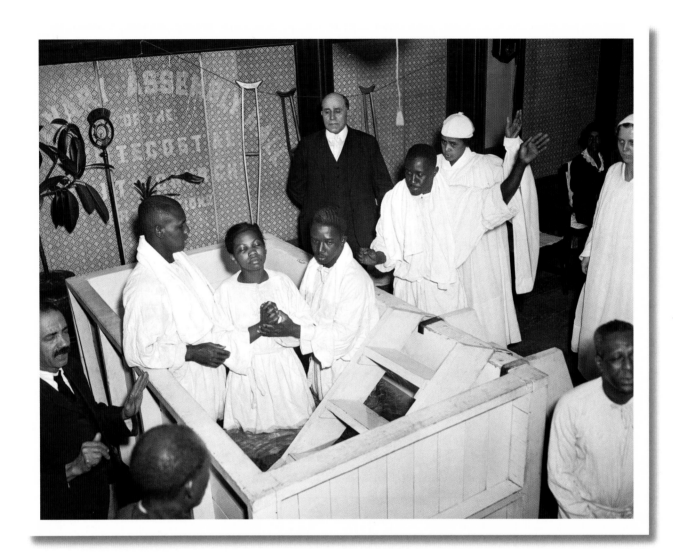

JAMES BALDWIN WORKED AS A YOUTH PREACHER AT A PENTECOSTAL CHURCH.
IN THIS PHOTOGRAPH FROM 1934, WORSHIPPERS PARTICIPATE IN A BAPTISM
CEREMONY AT ANOTHER PENTECOSTAL CHURCH IN HARLEM.

At age 14, James became a youth preacher at the Fireside Pentecostal Assembly. He was a powerful speaker. He never wrote his sermons. He always spoke from his heart. After three years, James gave up preaching. He felt that many people in the church were not being honest. "When we were told to love everybody, I had thought that that meant *everybody*. But no, it applied only to those who believed as we did, and it did not apply to white people at all," he explained.

James went to De Witt Clinton High School in the Bronx, a **borough** of New York City. One of his best friends was Emile Capouya. Another was Richard Avedon, who later became a famous photographer. The three boys worked together on the school magazine called *The Magpie*. James wrote many stories, poems, and plays. Under his yearbook picture, he listed as his future career goal "novelist-playwright."

IN HIGH SCHOOL, JAMES BALDWIN BECAME FRIENDS WITH RICHARD AVEDON, SHOWN HERE IN 1984. AVEDON IS ONE OF THE WORLD'S BEST-KNOWN PORTRAIT PHOTOGRAPHERS.

When James was 16, Emile introduced him to Beauford Delaney. Delaney was an artist in Greenwich Village, a neighborhood of artists in New York City. James later said Delaney was "the most important person in my life." He was "the first walking, living proof for me that a black man could be an artist," Baldwin said. "He taught me how to see, and how to trust what I saw. . . . And once you've had that experience you see differently."

After he graduated from high school in 1942, James Baldwin wanted to attend college. But he had to work to help support his family. He and his friend Emile found jobs laying railroad track for the U.S. Army in New Jersey.

The laws there were similar to the **Jim Crow laws** in the South. Under these laws, blacks were not allowed to enter public places used by whites. James Baldwin could not accept the unfair treatment. One night, a waitress told him, "We don't serve Negroes here." He picked up a mug of water and threw it at her. When Baldwin realized what he had done, he was frightened. "I saw . . . that my life, my real life, was in danger," he said, "and not from anything other people might do but from the hatred I carried in my own heart."

JIM CROW LAWS SEPARATED WHITES AND BLACKS IN PUBLIC PLACES, SUCH AS THIS MARYLAND RESTAURANT THAT ORDERED AFRICAN-AMERICANS TO ENTER THROUGH THE BACK DOOR. SUCH DISCRIMINATION ANGERED JAMES BALDWIN.

James Baldwin returned home in 1943. On July 29, his stepfather died. A few days later, a riot broke out in Harlem. A white policeman had shot a black soldier. Angry mobs set fires and broke into shops. James Baldwin later wrote that the streets were "a wilderness of smashed plate glass." He saw that the people of Harlem were as angry as his father had been. He was afraid that the "bitterness which had helped to kill my father could also kill me." He later wrote about these events and feelings in his essay "Notes of a Native Son."

James knew he had to leave Harlem. He rented a room in Greenwich Village, where he could be close to his family. He would also be able to follow his dream to become a writer.

ANGRY MOBS OVERTURNED THIS BURNING CAR DURING RIOTS THAT SWEPT HARLEM IN 1943. JAMES BALDWIN LATER WROTE AN ESSAY ABOUT THE EPISODE.

NEW YORK CITY'S VIBRANT GREENWICH VILLAGE ATTRACTED MANY ASPIRING
ARTISTS, ACTORS, MUSICIANS, AND WRITERS. JAMES BALDWIN MOVED THERE
IN 1943.

Greenwich Village

James Baldwin took many different jobs in Greenwich Village. He worked as a waiter, a dishwasher, and an elevator operator. After work, he went out with his friends. Then he returned to his room and wrote all night. He was writing a **novel** based on his childhood and his years as a preacher.

Baldwin became friends with many actors, artists, and writers in Greenwich Village. Through one friend, he met Richard Wright, the author of the best-selling book *Native Son*. Baldwin thought Wright was "the greatest black writer in the world."

Wright welcomed Baldwin into his home. He asked Baldwin about his novel and agreed to read the first part of the **manuscript.** The next day, Baldwin mailed it to him. Wright told his publisher about the young writer. The company gave Baldwin a grant of $500 and agreed to publish the novel when he finished it.

When Baldwin sent in the final manuscript, the publisher did not like it. Baldwin had worked hard, but he still had much to learn. He did not give up. He put the book aside and decided to write book reviews.

IN 1944, BALDWIN MET THE AFRICAN-AMERICAN AUTHOR RICHARD WRIGHT (ABOVE).

Baldwin's first review was of a book of short stories by a Russian writer. It was published in 1947 in a well-known magazine called *The Nation.* Soon, Baldwin was writing for several magazines. He wrote one book review each week.

The next year, he published his first essay, called "The Harlem Ghetto: Winter 1948." Baldwin wrote about the tension between African-Americans and Jewish people in Harlem. Baldwin believed that the two groups should work together. The magazine's editor called the essay "a masterpiece." But many Jewish people and African-Americans were angry at what Baldwin had written in *Commentary* magazine.

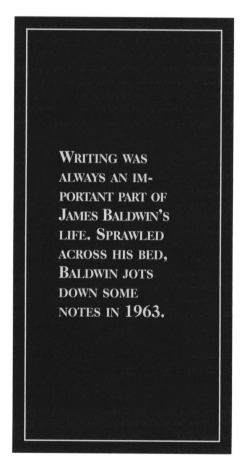

WRITING WAS ALWAYS AN IMPORTANT PART OF JAMES BALDWIN'S LIFE. SPRAWLED ACROSS HIS BED, BALDWIN JOTS DOWN SOME NOTES IN 1963.

Baldwin now felt ready to start another novel. This book was a love story between two men. At that time, there were few books about **homosexuals.** Many people did not approve of love relationships between people of the same sex. Baldwin believed that "love is love, rare and precious." He did not think that the color or sex of a person mattered at all.

During his life, Baldwin had love relationships with men and women. He was once engaged to marry his girlfriend, Grace. In high school, Baldwin had spoken to Emile Capouya about his attraction to other boys, which troubled and confused him at first. Now, he was ready to face and accept his true feelings.

Greenwich Village was filled with all types of people, but there were very few African-Americans living there. Just as many people treated blacks unfairly, many people also treated homosexuals unfairly. Baldwin was often chased and made fun of. He was thrown out of restaurants and mistreated by police. He felt bitterness and anger growing in him. Eugene Worth—Baldwin's best friend—had grown bitter, too. One day, he gave up hope. He killed himself by jumping off the George Washington Bridge.

Baldwin was losing hope, too. He was hurt that people did not accept him. He began to dislike himself. He began to doubt himself—as a man, an African-American, and a writer. "I no longer felt I knew who I really was," he wrote. "I had to get my head together to survive and my only hope of doing that was to leave America."

Baldwin bought a one-way ticket to Paris, France. "I didn't know what was going to happen to me in Paris, but I knew what was going to happen to me in New York," he said. "If I had stayed there, I would have gone under, like my friend on the George Washington Bridge." Baldwin left for Paris on November 11, 1948.

An American in Paris

James Baldwin felt free in Paris. Black Americans did not face the same problems there that they did in the United States. "I didn't have to prove anything to anybody," he said. "I could write, I could think, I could feel, I could walk, I could eat, I could breathe." One of the first people Baldwin saw in Paris was Richard Wright. Wright and his family had moved there two years before. Many other American writers were also living in Paris. Baldwin met writers Philip Roth, Norman Mailer, William Styron, Chester Himes, and James Jones.

Baldwin's first months in Paris were not easy. The $40 in his pocket lasted only three days. Jobs were hard to find.

Baldwin could not write for French magazines because he did not know the language. He had to sell his clothes to pay his hotel bill. He even had to sell his typewriter. He later had to borrow money from friends to buy it back.

Once Baldwin was arrested. An American friend had given him a bed sheet. Baldwin did not know that his friend had stolen the sheet from a hotel. The police found the sheet on Baldwin's bed. He spent several days in jail—including Christmas Day. When the judge discovered the mistake, he let Baldwin go. But Baldwin felt embarrassed and hurt. He later wrote about this event in his essay "Equal in Paris."

JAMES BALDWIN MOVED TO PARIS IN 1948. HE FELT COMFORTABLE IN THE FRENCH CAPITAL AND MET MANY WRITERS FROM THE UNITED STATES THERE.

In 1949, Baldwin met and fell in love with a Swiss man named Lucien Happersberger. After their romantic relationship ended, the two men remained lifelong friends. "We accepted each other exactly as we were," Baldwin said. "That's rare."

A Greek man named Themistocles James Hoetis invited Baldwin to write for his new magazine. The magazine was called *Zero.* Baldwin's essay "Everybody's Protest Novel" appeared in the first issue.

The essay was about *Uncle Tom's Cabin,* the book Baldwin had loved when he was young. Now he called it a "very bad novel." He said it was not art. Instead, he said it was just "protest writing" against slavery. Baldwin said that Richard Wright's book *Native Son* was protest writing, too. A protest writer speaks out against a problem in society. Baldwin believed that writers should do more than that. He believed that writers should help people understand themselves and become better human beings.

RICHARD WRIGHT'S *NATIVE SON* WAS RELEASED AS A MOVIE IN 1950. IT STARRED THE AUTHOR AS A YOUNG AFRICAN-AMERICAN WHO STRUGGLES WITH RACIAL INJUSTICE.

Wright was angry when he read the essay. He felt that Baldwin had betrayed him. Baldwin said he did not mean to hurt Wright at all. The two men never settled their quarrel. After Wright died, Baldwin wrote that he was sorry about the argument. Wright was his teacher, he said, and "always meant so much to me."

Baldwin spent a lot of time with his friends in Paris. He did not always spend enough time writing. In 1951, he and Happersberger left Paris so Baldwin could get some work done. They spent the winter in a small village in Switzerland. Baldwin was the first black man that some of the people there had ever seen. Some rubbed his hand to see if the color came off his skin. Others wanted to touch his hair. Baldwin later wrote about these experiences in his essay "Stranger in the Village."

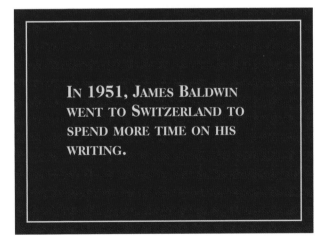

IN 1951, JAMES BALDWIN WENT TO SWITZERLAND TO SPEND MORE TIME ON HIS WRITING.

In just three months, Baldwin finished the novel he had shown to Richard Wright six years before. The book was called *Go Tell It on the Mountain.* The story is similar to Baldwin's own life story. The main character is John Grimes, a 14-year-old boy in Harlem. John becomes a preacher, just like his cruel stepfather. Baldwin said it was "the book I had to write if I was ever going to write anything else. I had to deal with what hurt me most. I had to deal, above all, with my father."

After sending the manuscript to his agent, Baldwin returned to Paris. A publisher in New York agreed to publish the book as long as he made some changes. Baldwin borrowed money from his friend, actor Marlon Brando, paid his hotel bill, and then set sail for New York. After only a few months in the United States, he returned to Europe. *Go Tell It on the Mountain* was published in May 1953. It was a great success. Baldwin's publisher wanted him to write another novel right away.

Baldwin decided to finish the love story he had started to write in Greenwich Village. The story, set in Paris, was based on a real murder that took place in New York City in 1943. All of the characters in the book were white. When Baldwin finished the manuscript, the publisher did not accept it. The editors wanted another book about blacks, and they were afraid to publish a book about homosexuals. A British publisher finally agreed to publish the book— and anything else that Baldwin would ever write. At the same time, a small American publisher also agreed to publish the book. *Giovanni's Room* was printed in the United States in 1956, and Baldwin won two important awards for it.

Baldwin was now well known as a fiction writer. Soon, he became famous as a writer of essays, too. In 1955, he published *Notes of a Native Son*. This book contains ten essays, including the one that made Richard Wright angry. Langston Hughes—the best-known black poet of the time—wrote about the book. He said that in Baldwin's essays "the thought becomes poetry, and the poetry **illuminates** the thought."

Living in France had helped Baldwin grow as a writer. It also helped him to see where he came from. "I am the grandson of a slave, and I am a writer. I must deal with both," he said. Nine years before, Baldwin had left the United States to "find out who he really was." As an African-American, he now needed to return to have a closer look.

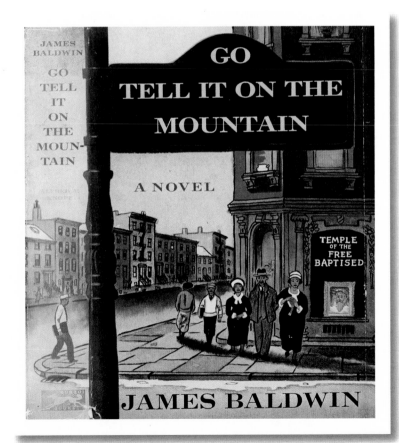

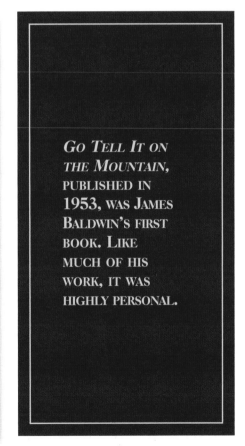

Go Tell It on the Mountain, published in 1953, was James Baldwin's first book. Like much of his work, it was highly personal.

"Witness to the Truth"

Baldwin heard about the many changes taking place in the southern United States. Blacks and whites were joining together to gain fair treatment for blacks. Baldwin had never visited the South, but now he wanted to go there. He felt it was his mission to "bear witness to the truth." "That's my responsibility," he said. "I write it all down."

In 1957, he went to Charlotte, North Carolina. Four black children there were attending all-white schools for the first time. Until then, white children and black children went to separate schools. A girl named Dorothy Counts was stoned and spat on by an angry crowd. A line of students blocked Gus Roberts from entering the school and called him names. Baldwin talked to these brave children. He wrote about Gus in an essay called "The Hard Kind of Courage." To protect the students, Baldwin did not name them, the school, or the town. The essay was later renamed "A Fly in Buttermilk."

A CROWD TAUNTS DOROTHY COUNTS AS SHE WALKS TO A PREVIOUSLY ALL-WHITE HIGH SCHOOL TO ENROLL IN 1957. BALDWIN WROTE ABOUT THE EVENT.

Next, Baldwin went to Atlanta, Georgia, to meet Martin Luther King Jr. King was a young preacher who was becoming an important leader. He told Baldwin he wanted to find peaceful ways to change society. The next Sunday, Baldwin went to hear King preach at his church. King helped Baldwin to join the **civil rights movement.**

BALDWIN MET MARTIN LUTHER KING JR. IN 1957. THE TWO MEN ARE SHOWN HERE AT CARNEGIE HALL IN 1968 AT A CELEBRATION TO HONOR W. E. B. DU BOIS.

When Baldwin returned from the South, he began writing about his experiences. "I met the most beautiful people I ever met in my life down there," he wrote. "I am proud of these people. . . . The country should be proud of them, too."

His book *Nobody Knows My Name: More Notes of a Native Son* was a best-seller. Soon, Baldwin was asked to speak on television. He was also invited to write more articles. One magazine asked him to write an article about a group called the Black Muslims. The Black Muslims had two leaders: Elijah Muhammad and Malcolm X. This group believed that black people should form their own nation. The leaders also believed in violence as a form of protest. Baldwin did not agree with their ideas. He believed that black and white Americans should learn to live together.

In 1962, Muhammad invited Baldwin to the Black Muslim headquarters in Chicago, Illinois. Baldwin wrote about their meeting in his essay "Letter from a Region in My Mind." The essay later became part of a book called *The Fire Next Time.* He added another essay to the book. The essay was a letter about pride and courage that he had written to his 15-year-old nephew, James.

Next, Baldwin traveled to Jackson, Mississippi. He met James Meredith, the first African-American to attend the University of Mississippi. He also visited civil rights leader Medgar Evers. This visit gave Baldwin the idea for his play *Blues for Mister Charlie.* The play is based on the true story of Emmett Till, a 14-year-old boy who was murdered for talking to a white woman.

JAMES BALDWIN DID NOT AGREE WITH THE VIOLENT BELIEFS OF MALCOLM X. THE BLACK MUSLIM LEADER WAS SHOT AND KILLED IN NEW YORK CITY ON FEBRUARY 21, 1965.

BALDWIN INTERVIEWED AND WROTE ABOUT BLACK MUSLIM LEADER ELIJAH MUHAMMAD, SHOWN HERE IN 1965.

In May 1963, riots broke out in Birmingham, Alabama. Hundreds of black children marching in the Children's Crusade were arrested. Police shot jets of water at thousands of protesters. When Baldwin saw what was happening, he got in touch with Robert Kennedy. Kennedy was the U.S. attorney general and the brother of President John F. Kennedy. Baldwin told him that the president needed to take action. That day, President Kennedy sent troops to calm the city. On May 17, Baldwin's picture was on the cover of *Time* magazine. The article praised him as a spokesperson for civil rights.

A few days later, Robert Kennedy asked Baldwin to meet him. Kennedy wanted help ending the riots in the United States. He asked Baldwin to invite several African-American leaders to a meeting. The meeting did not go well. The civil rights supporters were angry at the government. Kennedy said it was impossible to talk with them. After the meeting, Baldwin was afraid that Kennedy would no longer work for civil rights. But Kennedy continued to support Martin Luther King Jr. He also continued to ask the president to improve conditions in the South.

FIREFIGHTERS IN BIRMINGHAM, ALABAMA, SPRAY WATER AT AFRICAN-AMERICAN DEMONSTRATORS PROTESTING IN 1963.

Baldwin was in Paris during the planning of the March on Washington for Jobs and Freedom, which was to take place on August 28, 1963. He decided to organize his own march. Hundreds of black and white Americans marched down the streets of Paris. They delivered a **petition** to the U.S. embassy, asking to remove "all racial barriers in American life." Baldwin then flew to Washington, D.C., to join more than 200,000 blacks and whites in the civil rights march. He heard Martin Luther King Jr. make his famous speech, "I Have a Dream."

AFTER THE MARCH ON WASHINGTON FOR JOBS AND FREEDOM, JAMES BALDWIN STANDS AT THE LINCOLN MEMORIAL WITH ACTOR MARLON BRANDO (RIGHT), SINGER HARRY BELAFONTE (LEFT), AND ACTOR CHARLTON HESTON (FAR LEFT).

THE 1970S WERE A PRODUCTIVE TIME FOR JAMES BALDWIN. HE WROTE MANY BOOKS AT HIS FARMHOUSE IN THE SMALL FRENCH VILLAGE OF SAINT PAUL DE VENCE.

In March 1965, Baldwin joined another successful march, in Selma, Alabama. In the South, unfair laws kept many African-Americans from voting. These marchers wanted Congress to pass a bill that would allow millions of blacks to vote for the first time. In August, Congress finally passed the Voting Rights Act.

Baldwin's work for civil rights kept him from his typewriter. He began to spend time with friends in Istanbul, Turkey. There, he could focus on writing. Baldwin had been working on his novel *Another Country* for six years. He was able to finish it in several months in Turkey.

On April 4, 1968, Martin Luther King Jr. was killed in Memphis, Tennessee. At the time, Baldwin was working in Hollywood, California. He was writing a screenplay of *The Autobiography of Malcolm X* by Alex Haley. When he heard the news about King, he began to sob. For a time, he could not write at all. Then, he said to himself, "Martin never stopped, so I can't either."

In 1969, Baldwin returned to Istanbul to work. The next year he became ill. A friend took him to a small village in France called Saint Paul de Vence. Baldwin rented a large farmhouse there with gardens and lots of trees. Later, he bought the house, and it became his main home for the rest of his life.

Baldwin wrote many books in the next few years—including three books of essays, the novel *If Beale Street Could Talk,* and a children's story called *Little Man, Little Man: A Story of Childhood.* In 1979, Baldwin published his last and longest novel, *Just above My Head.* In this book, he writes about gospel, jazz, and blues music—the music that tells the story of African-Americans. He called it "a return to my own beginnings."

Later in life, Baldwin became a teacher. When Baldwin turned 60 years old, some friends gave him a birthday party. One of the many people there was the poet Maya Angelou. "I've learned one thing," he told his guests. "Never avoid the truth about yourself."

Baldwin spent his life telling the truth about himself and his country. His goal was to help all Americans—black and white—see the truth, too. "If we cannot understand ourselves," he wrote, "we will not be able to understand anything." Baldwin died on December 1, 1987, in France.

THIS PHOTOGRAPH OF JAMES BALDWIN WAS TAKEN IN 1985, TWO YEARS BEFORE HIS DEATH.

Timeline

1924 James Arthur Jones is born on August 2 in New York City.

1927 James Baldwin's mother, Emma Berdis Jones, marries David Baldwin, a factory worker and preacher. James is given his stepfather's last name.

1938 Baldwin becomes a preacher at the Fireside Pentecostal Assembly. He also begins classes at De Witt Clinton High School.

1942 Baldwin graduates from high school. He and his friend Emile Capouya work laying railroad track for the U.S. Army in New Jersey.

1943 David Baldwin dies on July 29. His funeral is held on Baldwin's 19th birthday. Baldwin moves to Greenwich Village.

1944 Baldwin meets Richard Wright, the author of *Uncle Tom's Children* and *Native Son.*

1947 Baldwin's first book review appears in *The Nation.*

1948 Baldwin's first essay, "The Harlem Ghetto: Winter 1948," and his first short story, "Previous Condition," are published in *Commentary* magazine. Baldwin moves to Paris, France.

1953 Baldwin's first novel, *Go Tell It on the Mountain,* is published.

1955 *Notes of a Native Son,* Baldwin's first book of essays, is published.

1956 Baldwin's second novel, *Giovanni's Room,* is published.

1957 In September, Baldwin makes his first trip to the southern United States. He meets Martin Luther King Jr.

1961 Baldwin publishes his second book of essays, *Nobody Knows My Name: More Notes of a Native Son.*

1962 Baldwin's essay about a visit with Black Muslim leader Elijah Muhammad appears in *The New Yorker.* His third novel, *Another Country,* the story of a jazz drummer, is published.

1963 Baldwin meets with U.S. attorney general Robert Kennedy. Baldwin joins the March on Washington for Jobs and Freedom. *The Fire Next Time* is published.

1965 Baldwin marches for African-American voting rights in Selma, Alabama.

1968 to 1979 Baldwin publishes several books: *Tell Me How Long the Train's Been Gone* (1968); *A Rap on Race* (with Margaret Mead) (1971); *No Name in the Street* and *One Day, When I Was Lost: A Scenario Based on Alex Haley's "The Autobiography of Malcolm X"* (1972); *A Dialogue* (with Nikki Giovanni) (1973); *If Beale Street Could Talk* (1974); *The Devil Finds Work* and *Little Man, Little Man: A Story of Childhood* (1976); and *Just above My Head* (1979).

1985 *The Price of the Ticket: Collected Nonfiction 1948–1985* is published.

1986 François Mitterand, the president of France, makes Baldwin a Commander of the French Legion of Honor.

1987 Baldwin dies of cancer on December 1 at his home in France. His funeral is held on December 8 at the Cathedral of St. John the Divine in New York City.

1989 *James Baldwin: The Price of the Ticket,* an award-winning film about the author's life, airs on the PBS television series *American Masters.*

2000 Howard University, in Washington, D.C., awards Baldwin an honorary doctoral degree of humane letters.

Glossary

**African-American
(AF-ri-kehn uh-MER-ih-kehn)**
An African-American is a black American whose ancestors came from Africa. James Baldwin grew up in Harlem, an African-American neighborhood in New York City.

borough (BUR-oh)
A borough is a section of a large city. The city of New York has five boroughs.

**civil rights movement
(SIV-il rites MOOV-muhnt)**
The civil rights movement was a series of events that took place during the 1950s and 1960s. Blacks and whites joined together to gain equal laws and equal rights for African-Americans.

essays (ESS-ayz)
An essay is a short piece of writing that presents the writer's personal point of view. James Baldwin wrote many essays during his career.

homosexuals (HO-mo-SEX-uels)
Homosexuals are men or women who share physical love with a person of the same sex. James Baldwin explored the subject of homosexuals in his work.

illuminate (ih-LOO-muh-nate)
To illuminate means to light up or make clear. Langston Hughes said that, in Baldwin's essays, "the thought becomes poetry, and the poetry illuminates the thought."

Jim Crow laws (Jim KRO LAWZ)
Jim Crow laws are laws that discriminate against African-Americans. These laws, which came into use in the southern United States in the 1880s, called for separation of the races in public places.

manuscript (MAN-yuh-skript)
A manuscript is a book or other written document that has not yet been published. A manuscript is the unedited draft of a book.

novel (NOH-vuhl)
A novel is a long written story. *Go Tell It on the Mountain, Giovanni's Room,* and *Another Country* are some of Baldwin's best-known novels.

petition (puh-TISH-uhn)
A petition is a written or spoken request. In the 1960s, James Baldwin and a group of other protesters in Paris delivered a petition to the U.S. embassy, asking to remove "all racial barriers in American life."

preacher (PREE-chur)
A preacher is a person who speaks in a church to convince others to act or share an idea. James Baldwin worked as a youth preacher.

slavery (SLAY-vur-ee)
Slavery is the practice of mistreating others by taking away their freedom and forcing them to work or act against their will. One of Baldwin's favorite books was a novel about slavery by Harriet Beecher Stowe titled *Uncle Tom's Cabin.*

Index

Further Information

Books

Gottfried, Ted. *James Baldwin: Voice from Harlem.* Danbury, Conn: Franklin Watts, 1997.

Rosset, Lisa. *James Baldwin.* New York: Chelsea House, 1989.

Steptoe, Michele. *African-American Voices.* Brookfield, Conn.: Millbrook, 1995.

Tackach, James. *James Baldwin.* San Diego, Calif.: Lucent Books, 1996.

Web Sites

Visit our homepage for lots of links about James Baldwin:

http://www.childsworld.com/links.html

Note to Parents, Teachers, and Librarians:
We routinely verify our Web links to make sure they're safe,
active sites—so encourage your readers to check them out!

About the Author

Deborah Cannarella is an author and editor of history and biography books for children. She also wrote *Zora Neale Hurston*, another book in the Journey to Freedom® series. Cannarella has also written several magazine articles and books for adults. She lives in Roxbury, Connecticut.